JOHN F. KENNEDY'S MOON SHOT

FRONT SEAT OF HISTORY: FAMOUS SPEECHES

TAMRA ORR

Published in the United States of America by Cherry Lake Publishing Group
Ann Arbor, Michigan
www.cherrylakepublishing.com

Reading Adviser: Marla Conn, MS, Ed., Literacy specialist, Read-Ability, Inc.
Content Adviser: Adam Fulton Johnson, PhD, Assistant Professor, History, Philosophy, and Sociology of Science, Michigan State University
Photo credits: © Robert Knudsen, White House Photographs, John F. Kennedy Presidential Library and Museum, Boston, cover, 6, 16; © Cecil Stoughton, White House Photographs, John F. Kennedy Presidential Library and Museum, Boston, 5, 15; © NASA Commons, AS11-40-5903, 8; © Independent Picture Service /Alamy Stock Photo, 11; © Library of Congress, LC-DIG-ds-07095, 12; © Papers of John F. Kennedy, Doodles, 22 August 1963, John F. Kennedy Presidential Library and Museum, Boston, 14; © NASA Commons, 87PC-0069, 8897361, 19; © JFK Library Army Signal Corps, PX65-108-CC18209, John F. Kennedy Presidential Library and Museum, Boston, 21; © NASA Commons, AS11-40-5877, 22; © NASA Commons, STS098-713a-016, 25; © NASA Commons, ISS018-E-00933, 26; © CrackerClips Stock Media/Shutterstock.com, 28 [top]; © intueri/Shutterstock.com, 28 [bottom]; © 3DSculptor/iStock.com, 29 [top]; © NASA Commons, S69-31739, 29 [bottom]

Cherry Lake Press is an imprint of Cherry Lake Publishing Group.

Library of Congress Cataloging-in-Publication Data has been filed and is available at catalog.loc.gov

Cherry Lake Publishing Group would like to acknowledge the work of the Partnership for 21st Century Learning, a Network of Battelle for Kids. Please visit http://www.battelleforkids.org/networks/p21 for more information.

Printed in the United States of America
Corporate Graphics

ABOUT THE AUTHOR

Tamra Orr is the author of more than 500 nonfiction books for readers of all ages. A graduate of Ball State University, she now lives in the Pacific Northwest with her family. When she isn't writing books, she is either camping, reading or on the computer researching the latest topics.

TABLE OF CONTENTS

CHAPTER 1

Fear of a "Red Moon"

In 1957, Russia, then known as the Soviet Union, sent up an unmanned spacecraft called Sputnik. *The United States was stunned that the Soviet Union had reached that level of technology. Four years later, on April 12, 1961, Yuri Gagarin, a Soviet astronaut, became the first person to go to space. Now the United States was more than surprised—it was embarrassed. It simply could not allow the Soviet Union to keep besting the United States in space technology. One of the first people to recognize the need to make drastic scientific changes and advances was President John F. Kennedy. He wanted the newly formed National Aeronautics and Space Administration (NASA) to focus on getting Americans to the Moon before anyone else. But he also knew that it was not going to be easy to sell the idea of a* **moon shot** *to the American public. A space program would take enormous funding, but Kennedy believed it was absolutely necessary to win the "space race."*

Kennedy delivered his speech at Rice University to a large crowd.

"Scoot over, David!" whispered Maya as she pushed on her big brother's shoulder. The football stadium's bleachers were crammed with people, and the Fishers were lucky they had found a spot to sit.

"There must be 35,000 people here," said Mrs. Fisher.

"At least," agreed Mr. Fisher. "I thought we'd never find a parking spot."

Maya looked around at the two levels of seating. She had never seen this many people gathered in one spot before. She and her family had already made plans to come to Rice University with David for freshman **orientation**. But at the time, they had no

The city of Houston, Texas, welcomed Kennedy as he made his way to Rice University.

idea that President Kennedy was going to be there! Now they were waiting for him to come to the **podium** and give a speech. Maya was excited—she was going to see the U.S. president in person!

Someone nearby grumbled about the heat. Maya agreed. It was incredibly hot and **humid**, even for September in Houston, Texas. Everywhere she looked, people were fanning themselves and wiping the sweat off of their foreheads. Even the politicians onstage looked pretty miserable.

“Think he’ll talk about going to the Moon?” Mrs. Fisher asked.

“He has to,” David said, nodding. “We can’t fall behind the Soviets.”

The man sitting behind them leaned forward and added, “We certainly don’t want a ‘red moon,’ do we?”

“I don’t get it,” said a woman next to Maya. “Why should we spend all of this money on exploring space when we could be using it to help people right here on Earth?”

Just then, the president walked to the podium out on the grass. The crowd went wild. People stood up, cheering and clapping, including the Fishers. All of the newspaper reporters were on their feet, their flashbulbs snapped like lightning as they took dozens of photos.

The Apollo 11 mission in 1969 landed astronauts Neil Armstrong and Edwin "Buzz" Aldrin on the Moon.

Maya's first thought was that he looked young for a president. The people behind Maya might not have agreed with President Kennedy on the space race. But everyone seemed to love him as a public figure.

"I am delighted to be here, and I'm particularly delighted to be here on this occasion," the president began. Maya grinned. So was she.

Talking to Congress

On May 25, 1961, Kennedy gave a speech to Congress about why the government needed to speed up its space exploration program. The president stated that he wanted the country to do more than send men to the Moon. He also wanted NASA to create a nuclear rocket, weather **satellites**, *and much more. It was a highly technical speech, full of numbers and statistics. It was meant to convince everyone that the United States was losing a race it very much needed to win.*

CHAPTER 2

"Why Does Rice Play Texas?"

President John F. Kennedy looked out over the crowd and smiled. "We meet at a college noted for knowledge, in a city noted for progress, in a state noted for strength, and we stand in need of all three. For we meet in an hour of change and challenge, in a decade of hope and fear, in an age of both knowledge and ignorance," he stated.

Maya was struck with what a powerful speaker the president was. She could see people in the audience smiling and nodding. They clearly liked the comments he made about the school and about Texas because everyone was clapping again.

Kennedy was elected president in 1960.

Kennedy married his wife Jackie in 1953.

The president did not hesitate to begin speaking about the nation's incredible accomplishments within science. He spoke about everything from the printing press, the steam engine, and electricity to airplanes, television, and nuclear power. Logically, it seemed space exploration must follow.

"This country of the United States was not built by those who waited and rested and wished to look behind them," he said. "This country was conquered by those who moved forward—and so will space." Kennedy then discussed how the space program would center on freedom and peace, not hostility or conquest. "We have vowed that we shall not see space filled with weapons of mass destruction, but with instruments of knowledge and understanding."

During his presidency, Kennedy's secretary cataloged all his notes, including his doodles.

Science, the president continued, was not good or bad. It was what people did with it that mattered. If the United States was leading the space program, he said, it could assure that "this new ocean will be a sea of peace" rather than "a new terrifying theater of war."

"I hadn't thought about space exploration as a matter of national security," Mr. Fisher said softly.

Kennedy had four children. They were some of the youngest to live in the White House.

The first American astronaut in space was Alan Shepard (left). Kennedy presented him with a Distinguished Service Medal in 1961.

"But why, some say, the Moon?" the president continued. "Why choose this as our goal?"

Maya knew that her parents had talked about this. She guessed that many Americans had too.

"And they may well ask, why climb the highest mountain?" President Kennedy added. With a grin, he then said, "Why does Rice play Texas?"

The crowd burst into laughter and applause. "Rice's football team's biggest rival is the University of Texas," David quietly explained to Maya.

Kennedy sure knew how to win over a crowd.

The Space Race

When the Soviet Union launched Sputnik *in 1957, the race to reach space kicked into gear. In 1958, the United States launched* Explorer I *and created NASA. In April 1961, the Soviet Union beat America again by sending the first person into space to orbit Earth. The United States followed the next month by sending its first astronaut into space. From that point forward, the United States surged ahead in the space race, creating the successful Apollo program.*

CHAPTER 3

The "Greatest Adventure"

"I understand his point," Mr. Fisher admitted. "But going into space seems like one of the toughest goals any nation could have."

"We choose to go to the Moon in this decade and do the other things," President John F. Kennedy continued, "not because they are easy, but because they are hard . . . because that challenge is one that we are willing to accept, one we are unwilling to postpone, and one which we intend to win." He explained how much the nation had already achieved, such as the testing of **booster rockets** and rocket engines, as well as dozens of satellites.

John Glenn became the first American to orbit the Earth. His ship, Friendship 7, took off in February 1962.

However, Kennedy confessed that the United States was not keeping up in terms of space exploration. “To be sure, we are behind and will be behind for some time in manned flight,” he said. “But we do not intend to stay behind, and in this decade, we shall make up and move ahead.”

"And the cost?" a man sitting behind the Fishers grumbled to himself. As if hearing him, Kennedy explained how a number of new companies, plus tens of thousands of jobs, would come from a nationwide focus on science. He said that the price of going to the Moon would break down to only about 50 cents a week for every person in the country. The man stopped his grumbling.

"Many years ago, the great British explorer George Mallory, who was to die on Mount Everest, was asked why did he want to climb it. He said, 'Because it is there,'" said President Kennedy. "Well, space is there, and we're going to climb it. And the Moon and the planets are there, and new hopes for knowledge and peace are there. And therefore, as we set sail . . . we ask God's blessing on the most hazardous and dangerous and greatest adventure on which man has ever embarked."

Kennedy's inaugural address included the famous line "Ask not what your country can do for you; ask what you can do for your country."

Astronaut Buzz Aldrin's bootprint on the Moon's surface is a famous image.

The roar of applause as the president finished his speech was incredible. It was less than 20 minutes, but it had made an impact. Maya had goosebumps, and she was pretty sure she was not the only one. After all, America was going to the Moon!

A Moon Landing

On July 20, 1969, Neil Armstrong stepped on the Moon's surface. He was the first human being to do so. The entire world was glued to their television sets. They heard the astronaut say the famous words, "This is one small step for man, one giant leap for mankind." One person who did not see it was President Kennedy. Tragically, he had been **assassinated** *on November 22, 1963, a little more than a year after his speech at Rice University. In his honor, the nation had worked to make Kennedy's wish come true. The United States had reached the Moon by the end of the decade, before anyone else.*

CHAPTER 4

More Adventures Await

Arlington, Texas, 2018. A phone rang in an apartment. David shook his head as he made his way over to the phone. He had a feeling who it might be.

"Hi, David, it's me." A voice on the other end chimed in before he could say hello. David smiled.

"Hi, Maya."

"Did you watch that documentary on the International Space Station last night?" Maya asked her brother. He chuckled. She had texted him three reminders this week alone.

"I did. And it was great," he replied. "It made me think back to that day at Rice University."

The International Space Station (ISS) was photographed in 2001.

"Me too," Maya said. "I wonder what President John F. Kennedy would have thought about the ISS."

"I think he would have loved it," David replied. "But I think he would have been shocked that part of it came from Russia. He was so worried about the threat of the Soviet Union."

Astronauts at the ISS perform space walks to do maintenance on the station.

"I know!" said Maya. "I thought about all of that when the documentary showed President Ronald Reagan asking the nation to support the construction of the space station. He was doing what Kennedy did."

"I learned a lot from the show," said Maya. "It took 10 years and 30 missions to complete it. Think of the pressure those scientists must have felt!"

"Do you think President Kennedy could have ever imagined any of this would be possible?" wondered David.

"I'm just excited that we've gotten to witness some of the changes," Maya replied.

"Even if we have a little gray hair and some wrinkles," David finished with a smile. "Who knows what 'greatest adventures' still await."

Renewing the Race

More than 50 years from when President Kennedy announced the nation would go to the Moon, Vice President Mike Pence said almost the same thing. In a speech before the National Space Council in 2019, Pence stated the country's renewed commitment to get back to the Moon. The goal is to get U.S. astronauts on the Moon by 2024 and eventually to the surface of Mars.

TIMELINE

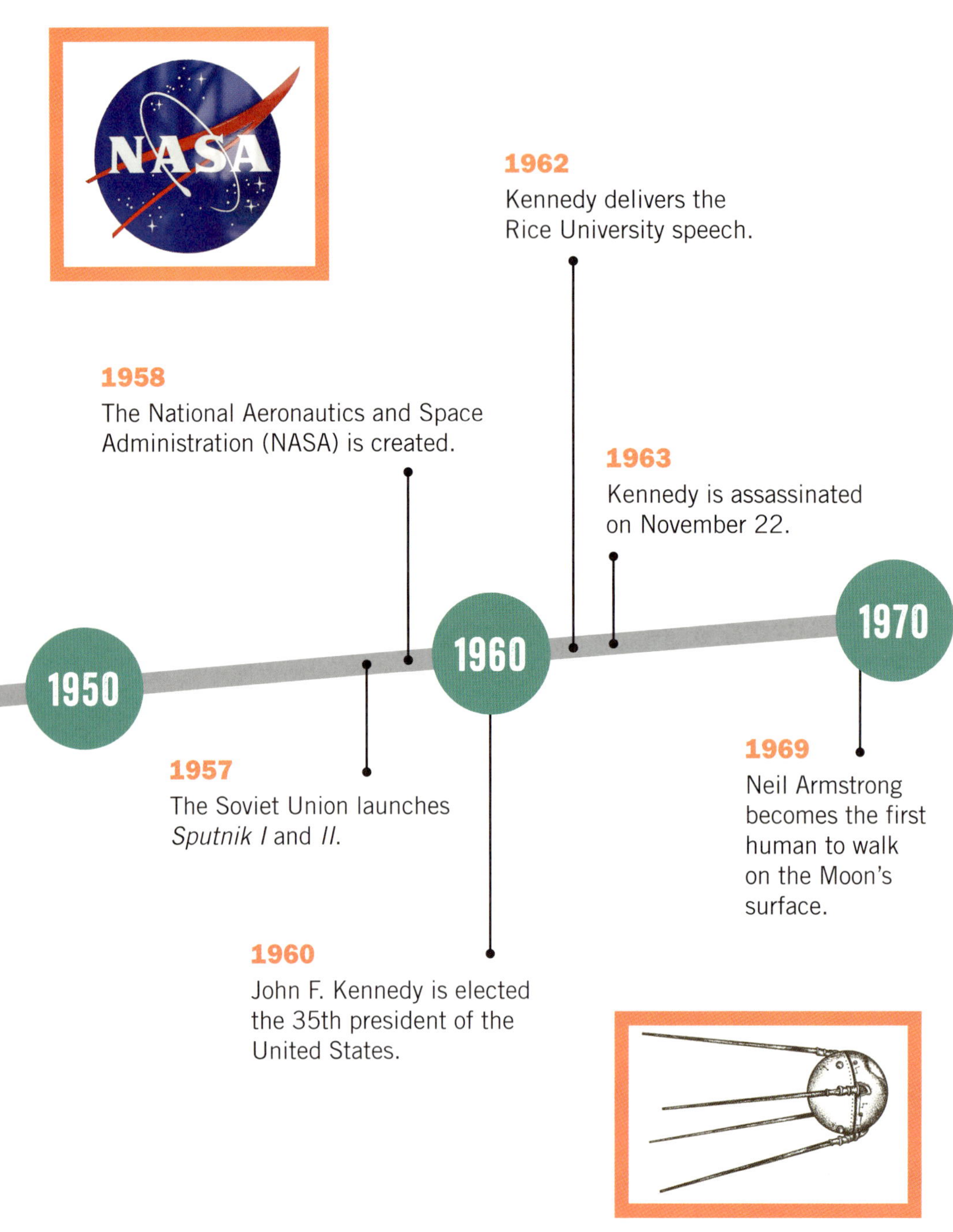

1957
The Soviet Union launches *Sputnik I* and *II*.

1958
The National Aeronautics and Space Administration (NASA) is created.

1960
John F. Kennedy is elected the 35th president of the United States.

1962
Kennedy delivers the Rice University speech.

1963
Kennedy is assassinated on November 22.

1969
Neil Armstrong becomes the first human to walk on the Moon's surface.

1984

President Ronald Reagan calls for the creation of an International Space Station (ISS).

1980

1990

2000

1998

Construction of the ISS begins. It was completed in 2011. The station continues to add new components.

Speech Highlight

"We choose to go to the Moon. We choose to go to the Moon in this decade and do the other things, not because they are easy, but because they are hard, because that goal will serve to organize and measure the best of our energies and skills, because that challenge is one that we are willing to accept, one we are unwilling to postpone, and one which we intend to win, and the others, too."

Read the full speech at https://er.jsc.nasa.gov/seh/ricetalk.htm.

Research and Act

Research

Think of all that has happened since President John F. Kennedy gave his speech at Rice University in 1962. Research the main events in space exploration that have occurred between his speech and today.

Act

Create a timeline of events from 1962 through today, marking some of the biggest events in space exploration. You can use the timeline on pages 28 and 29 to get you started. Go 25 to 50 years in the future, and make your best guesses at what you think will occur during those years.

Further Reading

Brinkley, Douglas. *American Moonshot: John F. Kennedy and the Great Space Race.* New York, NY: Harper, 2019.

Huddleston, Emma. *Exploring Kennedy Space Center.* Lake Elmo, MN: Focus Readers, 2020.

Kawa, Katie. *Before John F. Kennedy Was President.* New York, NY: Gareth Stevens Publishing, 2018.

Moore, Shannon Baker. *John F. Kennedy's Assassination Rocks America.* Mankato, MN: Child's World, 2018.

GLOSSARY

assassinated (uh-SAS-uh-nate-id) murdered for political reasons

booster rockets (BOOST-ur RAH-kits) engines that give thrust during a launch

humid (HYOO-mid) high level of moisture in the air

moon shot (MOON SHAHT) a spacecraft mission to the Moon

orientation (or-ee-uhn-TAY-shuhn) a set of activities that get you ready to take part in something new

podium (POH-dee-uhm) a stand with a surface for holding papers, for use by a person giving a speech

satellites (SAT-uh-lites) objects that orbit the planet and relay communications or data back to Earth

INDEX